Field Guide

For Focusing on Photography

And Grasping Depth of Field

Bryan Serpa Stedman

ISBN: 148014746X
ISBN-13: 978-1480147461

TO THOSE AROUND ME:

Your support and generosity over the years made this book possible.

Set backs were supported and progress continued.

CONTENTS

ACKNOWLEDGMENTS

Thank you to all who have helped me improve technically with photography. And special thanks to the opportunities that have let me share my work with others: Typically through free mediums.

And a special thanks to a teacher, who's methods appeared chaotic at best – but the realization of this book would not have been possible: Edward Fishback.

CHAPTER 1
What Now? <u>AND</u> Basic Concepts

What to think:

The intent of this book is to operate with the Manual Mode of your camera; that is not to say you can not adapt the pages here and utilize the other settings (automatic will be of zero use); for brevity I will always refer to the Manual Mode setting.

Vocabulary:

- **Light** is what allows the photograph to be made and appear (or not to appear) on paper. *Dark* is the absence of Light and *bright* is the abundance of light. The camera settings adjust for these effects – such is life, there are pro's and cons.

- **Aperture = f-stop = $^1/_f$** = This is how "open" the shutter will be during exposure (or how much of the lens will be exposed). It is also the controlling factor for Depth of Field: the limits of a lens's ability to record in focus. Essentially if the aperture is wide open (f/5.6) and you focus on something very close, everything behind (possibly in front as well) will have a blurrring effect. This is because a lens can only focus on one point and sharpness will decay (or blurrr will increase). Consider your eyes and the amount of squinting in relation to this concept.

- **Shutter Speed = $^1/_{shutter\ speed}$** = This is how "quickly" the shutter will open and close. Like aperture it contributes to *how* much light is let in and exposed. With aperture the amount of light that may get in is set! If the aperture is a small size and yet the speed is very slow (staying open for a long time) then a dark scene may actually appear bright. The opposite is true, a large aperture and fast shutter speed may make a very bright scene appear balanced. And with experimentation, the two scenarios may balance out and yield equal results (minus the finer details of what is and isn't in focus). Again, consider being outside in the sun. You could squint or blink rapidly and have the same amount of light enter.

- **ISO** can be described as a factor that compensates for the quality of light. Tied to a specific film type, your digital camera's power expands greatly: Having the equivalent ability to shoot a variety of film with a slight adjustment. The beauty is that increasing the ISO for a shot (preset aperture and shutter speed) makes a dark scene into a well-lit scene. The only draw back is a *graininess* effect occurs. Which may just work well for certain effects. Adjusting ISO becomes handy when light is low and handheld shots are all that are available. ISO maybe broken down into a range of: 100 is appropriate for bright and abundant light sources, while1600+ is utilized in low light (poor quality) situations. More later.

Before we proceed:

Let me explain my aim (pardon the pun), simply it is that we must define the limits of the tool you are using. By accepting the limits of the camera and operating within them: Error will be trivial and you will enhance your photographs by working outside the range of the simple Automatic Mode. The final result is an understanding of what will occur when you reach the near limits – average is so average.

Consider:

Each box represents a photograph you would like to take (either 3 different scenes):

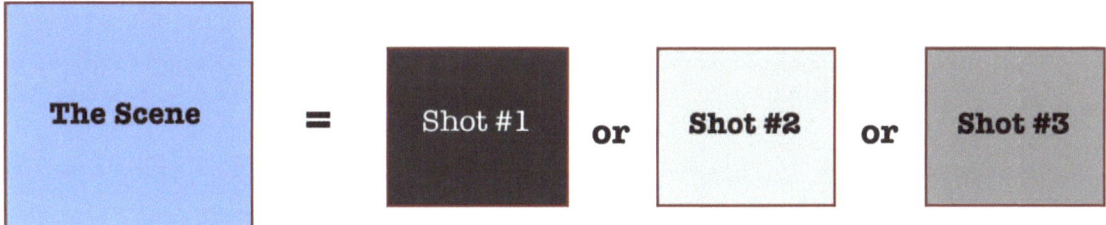

Figure 1: A shot attempt

Based on the settings (determined by the vocabulary terms above) the result is shown above where Shot #1 is very dark; Shot #2 is very light; and Shot #3 is in between. This can even happen in Automatic Mode because the setting tricks the camera – even then you must understand what the camera is assuming to avoid poor results.

What does this mean?

First, I must apologize if you are fearful of mathematics and science but what is presented here is the key to this manual (the goal is to simplify concepts to the critical information and by retaining those parts success will be easy). Our endeavor is comparable to learning to fly a plane before driving a car. The process is very complex when all the variables are considered at one time – we are building a foundation, which with work and dedication will result in flapping our wings to fly.

Please try to consider that the photograph is the end result of an experiment, described by a phrase:

Amount of Light Needed is based on **ISO** and $^1/_f$ and $^1/_{\textbf{shutter speed}}$

The order is based on which settings you choose prior to the "Click."

For now above is the correct order of operation.

Now what if we treat the above as an equation that can be written as:

$$\text{Amount of Light Needed} = \text{ISO} + {}^{1}/_{f} + {}^{1}/_{\text{shutter speed}}$$

A Starting Point:

So, if we read this equation as a recipe, such that the settings are based on:

- ISO, is based on the light conditions (for a "rough" idea of what will be selected later) we are able to preselect the maximum quality of the shot (1600 may work most of the time but yields that grainy effect). ISO then controls the remaining settings:

- Leaving only certain ${}^{1}/_{f}$ (apertures) available THAT

- Can combine with ${}^{1}/_{\text{shutter speed}}$ AND result in a *QUALITY PHOTOGRAPH*.

If you understand the *RANGE* that these variables operate in and their use, you then can begin to make combinations to generate photographs.

Don't fret; it will take much practice and experience to properly analyze the scene for the optimum output. But now we have a starting point. The goal should be that each scene is becoming easier to shoot and analyze. So maybe it will take 5 shots to dial in the settings and later 3 and maybe never 1 shot. But only by reviewing your plan as it was executed; can your skills will improve.

Basic Trouble Shooting - Figure 1: Shot #1 Too Dark?

Why?

- Possibly the Aperture Number/Size was too large (meaning it didn't open enough) like f/36 and f/16 would have been more appropriate (the reverse works if the shot was too bright) and the photographer must be aware that as the aperture *opens up*, there is an issue with Depth of Field (discussed later).
- Possibly the Shutter Speed was too *fast* like 1/200 and closed too soon, not letting the right amount of light in. Maybe you needed to be at 1/30 (careful because as the number below the "one" gets smaller the shutter is staying open longer and a possibility of "hand-shake" may blurrr the photo).
- Possibly the ISO was too low, say 100 when 400 was more appropriate (careful again, as the ISO number gets bigger the shot will become grainy; but only at 800 and above is it significant)
- And possibly it is the combination of all of them. Adjusting one setting to all of them may improve the shot.

REMEMBER: AS THE APERTURE NUMBER INCREASES THE LIGHT LET IN DECREASES and AS SHUTTER SPEED NUMBER INCREASES THE LIGHT LET IN ALSO DECREASES. Ultimately, a larger aperture is like squinting AND a larger shutter speed is like blinking.

That's it, that's the approach you need to take. Simply pick one setting and then the others until the photo turns out the way you like (pages to come will make you more efficient at the process). As one setting is changed it has an effect on the others (depending on the light).

> *Note: This might be a good spot to switch back to Automatic so you pick at least one of the settings and see how the camera's selection compares to what you would have done.*

An example,

1. After viewing the scene you will have a rough idea of the light and the photograph you'd like to capture.
2. Initially you should start at ISO 200, shutter 125, and aperture f/10
3. But the shot turns out dark (ignoring Depth of Field for now)

What can you do?

1. Since the shot is too dark, we know we can tweak:
    a. Aperture
    b. ISO
    c. Shutter Speed
2. Changing the Aperture is best because a slower Shutter Speed may result in a blurry photo (hand-shake). The ISO change may also be appropriate but as ISO exceeds 400 (ISO 800 and 1600) that grainy effect is apparent.
3. So if switching from ISO 200 to 400 fixes the shot that is the easiest choice.
4. Otherwise, we may have to change the Aperture from f/10 to f/5.6
5. And of course the Shutter Speed can be slowed from 1/125 to 1/60, to safely avoid that hand-shake.
6. If it is assumed that the picture failed to turn out with the proposed changes, a combination of changes will be needed, until the work is done.

Except one issue remains: **_Depth of Field_**. As the aperture opens up then you need to be aware that the shot will only appear within a range and anything appearing outside will have *some* amount of blurrr.

An Internet search will yield sites with online calculators, giving the flexibility to input distances and settings of previous or future shots and see where the optimum place for an object will be. Try: www.dofmaster.com or stay tuned for my own spread sheet style calculator.

CHAPTER 2
An Explanation on How to Proceed

Are you in *MANUAL MODE*?

⟶ *This book works under the basic assumption you have some familiarity (or are learning about) the settings for operating in the Manual Mode of your camera.*

In this book you will find a series of exercises and worksheets.

The fact you are not in AUTOMATIC MODE of your camera is critical; from there you can utilize the sheets within your own comfort zone – try letting the camera set Aperture or Shutter Speed AND you can select the other option. Or go for all MANUAL MODE and experiment in that fashion (which will be the primary steps in this book).

The concept is to complete the exercises and worksheets **AND** compare your notes to the resulting photograph. You *SHOULD* analyze what works in the photograph and doesn't work – you should NOT PROCEED without total understanding (and possibly regenerating the work with a successful outcome).

The benefit of TRIAL and ERROR is that learning from errors will lead to successful pictures in the future. This is the key, just accepting something (as wrong) and not finding the cause is camouflage and will only work part of the time (and I guarantee it will be the least opportune time when failure lurks out).

The goal is to be proficient and generate quality ALL (well the majority) of the time. Perfection should be gold-standard.

CHAPTER 3
More Explanation and How to Proceed

The Worksheets:

This book contains 4 main worksheets — starting from the most basic of exercises to a form that will allow you to record/organize your thoughts before and after the shot. As you move ahead you will encounter the blank sheet; followed by a completed sheet and a series of photographs for reference. With luck you will be able to study the sheet and photographs and then make your own pictures. From there you will need to repeat the analysis and you may benefit from reviewing what is included in this book (earlier pages and the photos).

1. Sheet Type I - Basic Worksheet:

Test No. ____ ISO _____		Date/Location:
1/f	**shutter**	**Notes:**
Low f = ...		
Test 1		
Test 2		
Test 3		
Mid f = ...		
Test 1		
Test 2		
Test 3		
High f = ...		
Test 1		
Test 2		
Test 3		

Steps:
a. Select the ISO and record this Number. This will be the initial estimate based on your "feel" of what the light conditions are.
b. Based on the ISO, select the f-stop; again determined by light conditions you see.
c. Finally, take a shot at a specified shutter speed (try to balance the light meter).
d. Make notes and repeat the shutter speed selection to improve the photograph.
e. Move on to a new scene where you will need to adjust the f-stop.

2. Sheet Type II – Setting Adjustments

Picture No.			Date:		
Picture Idea:			Conditions:		
			Location:		
Initial ISO:					
1/f :					
Shutter spd:					
Light Meter Test?					
Adjustments:	ISO	1/f	Shutter Sp.	Histogram Accptble?	
Shot 2		const.			
Notes:					

Steps:
  a. Record the basic information for the photograph you will take.
  b. Select an ISO (similar to the first exercise).
  c. Select the f-stop and shutter speed.
  d. Take a light reading – is it acceptable?
     a. Yes – take the photograph.
     b. No – take photograph and make/record adjustments in "shot 2" adjustments.
  e. After taking the second photograph – look at the histograms (graph of light balance).
  f. Review and understand what worked and didn't work.

3. Sheet Type III – Log Sheet (abbreviated)

Selection of:				Light Meter Reading?	Post Shot:	
"f"	ISO	shutter speed	Basis of Selections:	Desc. Loc. & Rding:	Replicate Histogrm?	
	100 200 400 800 1600			-2 . . 1 . . + . . 1 . . 2		

Steps:
  a. Record the basic information for the photograph you will take. (not shown above)
  b. Building on what has been accomplished to this point (and looking back at the text and other reference materials), we will need to:
    a. Judge the light.
    b. Select the f-stop. <f-stop is critical b/c it will determine the DoF>
    c. Select the ISO. <As ISO increases the appearance becomes grainy>
    d. Select Shutter Speed.
    e. Record the resulting Light Meter reading.
    f. Take the photograph.
    g. Sketch the Histogram and review your choices.

The purpose behind the tables and the charting is to document the work you are doing AND later return and evaluate the product of a day's shoot. Much of this information can be recorded with the camera and deduced later. But this approach allows you to (1) work in the moment and (2) minimize the extra learning required to capturing the best photographs.

CHAPTER 4
Example Shots & Analysis: Basis for Forms

Shot No.	Description	ISO	1/f	1/shutter speed
Fully Automatic	Key on black	400?		
1	table top mix of	100	1/8	100
2	sun & shade,	100	1/5.6	100
3	grey pavement	100	1/8	50

Notes: This group of photographs was taken in my backyard. The ground is concrete (neutral gray) and the table top black, while the key itself is reflective silver. The following things were considered prior to shooting:

→ What is the overall light like? What is the scene like and what do I want to appear?
→ From there I took the first shot – set on automatic, as a control for comparison.
→ What must be considered is if the vision you have will actually appear do to the uncontrollable factors of: bright vs. dark; speed of object; effect; etc.

Over all, the light was not harsh, but was mixed – the table was partially in direct light and partially shaded. The key was in the direct light. The photographic decision was to emphasize the "key" and let it reside on the dark table. Further, the lighter (than the table) concrete would serve as a nice background.

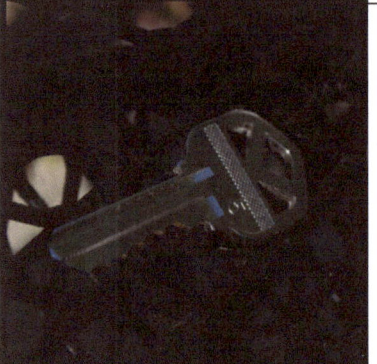

Example Shot Fully Automatic

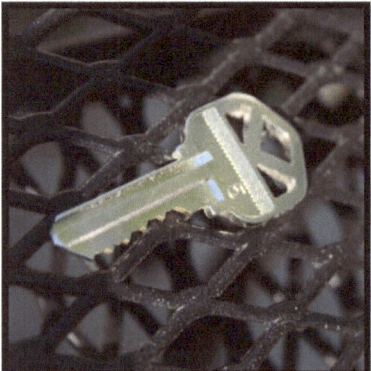

Example Shot 2

Results

Fully Automatic: The fully automatic shot appears too dark b/c the sensor took the reading from the key only; resulting in a reading that considered the scene overly bright. Thus the whole shot is much too dark.

Shots 1, 2 & 3: In the case of these three shots, the light meter was not utilized – Shot 1 was a judgment call. I selected 100 ISO b/c the light was ample; aperture as 1/8 to balance the DoF with the amount of light entering. Finally the shutter speed was selected as 1/100 b/c the object is at rest & I felt I would have reasonable results from the other settings.

The other shots were based on similar logic.

Which shot would you select?

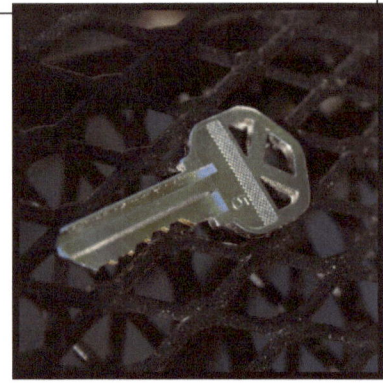

Example Shot 1

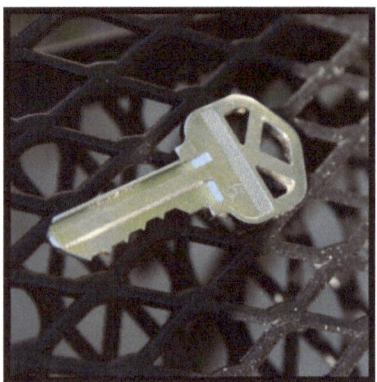

Example Shot3

CHAPTER 5
Example Shots & Analysis: Histograms

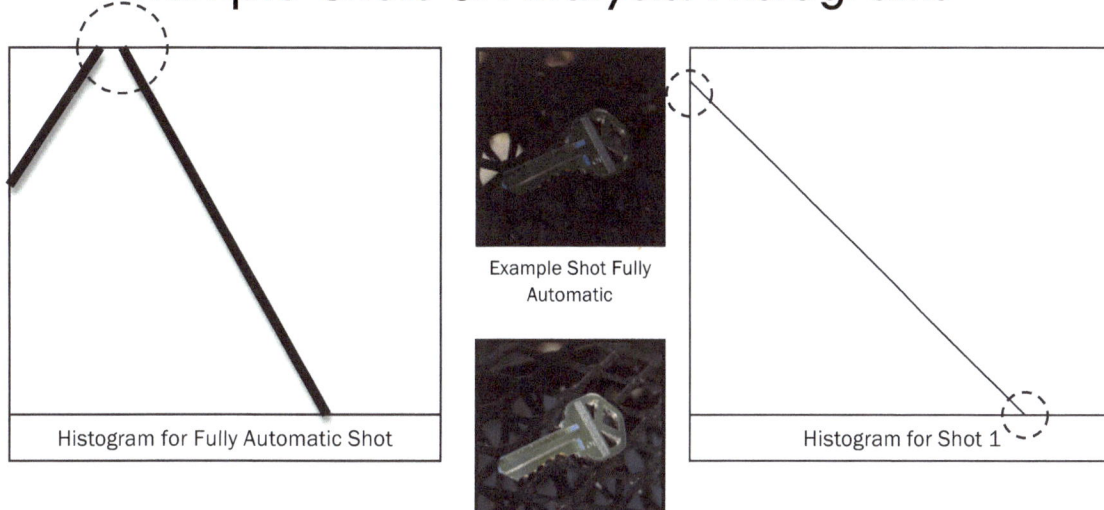

Histogram for Fully Automatic Shot

Example Shot Fully Automatic

Example Shot 1

Histogram for Shot 1

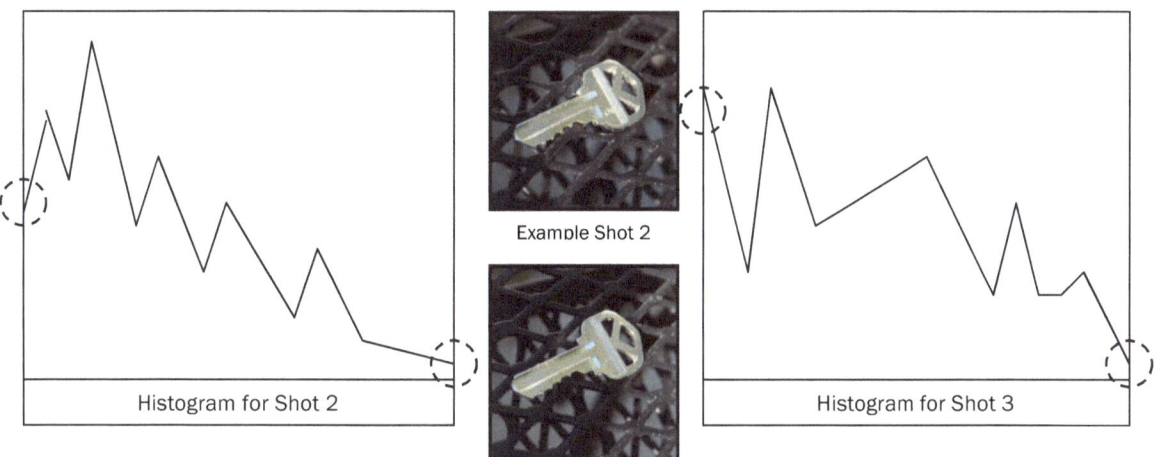

Histogram for Shot 2

Example Shot 2

Example Shot3

Histogram for Shot 3

The circles indicate the problem areas – in this case too much bright light was let in and the dark was off as well. Interestingly, Shot 1 is relatively acceptable – and all could be modified (with acceptable improvement) with Photoshop. Of special note, is that the shot with the automatic setting did not result in the best recorded.

The graphs are simplified versions that highlight what the camera captured. As you can see all the photos have dark regions where detail is nearly lost and the key is varies in brightness – in this case the key is overly bright.

APPENDIX
ADDITIONAL WORKSHEETS

Sheet Type Ia

Test No. ____	ISO _____	Date/Location:
1/f	shutter	Notes:
Low f = ...		
Test 1		
Test 2		
Test 3		
Mid f = ...		
Test 1		
Test 2		
Test 3		
High f = ...		
Test 1		
Test 2		
Test 3		

Test No. ____	ISO _____	Date/Location:
1/f	shutter	Notes:
Low f = ...		
Test 1		
Test 2		
Test 3		
Mid f = ...		
Test 1		
Test 2		
Test 3		
High f = ...		
Test 1		
Test 2		
Test 3		

Sheet Type Ib

integral Art concepts

Created By: B. Serpa

Page No. _____

Sheet Type I - Initial Practice Sheet for Learning Flow of Light and Variables with an SLR

Test No. _____ ISO _____

1/f	shutter	Date/Location:	Notes:
Low f = ...			
Sun			
Shade			
Mix			
Mid f = ...			
Sun			
Shade			
Mix			
High f = ...			
Sun			
Shade			
Mix			

Test No. _____ ISO _____

1/f	shutter	Date/Location:	Notes:
Low f = ...			
Test 1			
Test 2			
Test 3			
Mid f = ...			
Test 1			
Test 2			
Test 3			
High f = ...			
Test 1			
Test 2			
Test 3			

Test No. _____ ISO _____

1/f	shutter	Date/Location:	Notes:
Low f = ...			
Sun			
Shade			
Mix			
Mid f = ...			
Sun			
Shade			
Mix			
High f = ...			
Sun			
Shade			
Mix			

Hints [Assuming a 18 - 55mm Lens]

1/f :		
3.5/4/5.6	wide open	max Dpth fld
11/15/2018	mid way	Midway
22/29/36	small open	least Dfield
Shutter:		
1200+	Super Duper Fast	Capture Movement (freeze)
500	Still Fast	
125	Med. Rng.	
30	Slow - for hand held	Be Still - lean on tree (or me)
0'8 sec	Sloooow	Tripod Mandatory

Instructions:
1. Select a Shot - Visualize and Make an Initial Judgement of the Light and Environment
2. Step 1 will decide which 1/f is most appropriate - log this.
3. Step 2 or 1/f will now determine the ISO and shutter speed.
   a. ISO = based on quality/quantity of light, v.low=1600 to grt=100
   b. shutter, consider movement in shot and effect desired, coupled with lighting
4. Take the shot and make general notes.
5. Repeat 1 to 4 to improve or expirment with settings.
6. Repeat 5 for varioius 1/f.

Last Revised: 9/13/2010

Worksheet No. 1

integral Art concepts

Sheet Type I - Initial Practice Sheet for Learning Flow of Light and Variables with an SLR

Page No. _____

Test No. ____	ISO	shutter	Date/Location:	Notes:
1/f				
Low f = ...				
Test 1				
Test 2				
Test 3				
Mid f = ...				
Test 1				
Test 2				
Test 3				
High f = ...				
Test 1				
Test 2				
Test 3				

Test No. ____	ISO	shutter	Date/Location:	Notes:
1/f				
Low f = ...				
Sun				
Shade				
Mix				
Mid f = ...				
Sun				
Shade				
Mix				
High f = ...				
Sun				
Shade				
Mix				

Test No. ____	ISO	shutter	Date/Location:	Notes:
1/f				
Low f = ...				
Sun				
Shade				
Mix				
Mid f = ...				
Sun				
Shade				
Mix				
High f = ...				
Sun				
Shade				
Mix				

HintS [Assuming a 18 - 55mm Lens]

1/f :		
3.5/4/5.6	wide open	max Dpth fld
11/15/2018	mid way	Midway
22/29/36	small open	least Dfield
Shutter:		
1200+	Super Duper Fast	
500	Still Fast	Capture Movement (freeze)
125	Med. Rng.	
30	Slow - for hand held	Be Still - lean on tree (or me)
0"8 sec	Sloooow	Tripod Mandatory

Instructions:
1. Select a Shot - Visualize and Make an Initial Judgement of the Light and Environment
2. Step 1 will decide which 1/f is most appropriate - log this.
3. Step 2 or 1/f will now determine the ISO and shutter speed.
   a. ISO = based on quality/quantity of light, v.low=1600 to grt=100
   b. shutter, consider movement in shot and effect desired, coupled with lighting
4. Take the shot and make general notes.
5. Repeat 1 to 4 to improve or expirment with settings.
6. Repeat 5 for varioius 1/f.

Last Revised: 9/13/2010

Sheet Type II

Contact Info: serpa.c68322@gmail.com

www.flickr.com/photos/polite_engr

Last Revised: 9/13/2010

integral Art concepts

Sheet Type II – Experiments with Set 1/f and Variable Shutter/ISO

Page No. ___

Picture No. 　 Date:
Picture Idea: 　 Conditions:
　 Location:

Initial ISO:
1/f :
Shutter spd:

Light Meter Test?

Adjustments:	ISO	1/f const.	Shutter Sp.	Histogram Accptble?
Shot 2				

Notes:

Picture No. 　 Date:
Picture Idea: 　 Conditions:
　 Location:

Initial ISO:
1/f :
Shutter spd:

Light Meter Test?

Adjustments:	ISO	1/f const.	Shutter Sp.	Histogram Accptble?
Shot 2				

Notes:

Picture No. 　 Date:
Picture Idea: 　 Conditions:
　 Location:

Initial ISO:
1/f :
Shutter spd:

Light Meter Test?

Adjustments:	ISO	1/f const.	Shutter Sp.	Histogram Accptble?
Shot 2				

Notes:

Picture No. 　 Date:
Picture Idea: 　 Conditions:
　 Location:

Initial ISO:
1/f :
Shutter spd:

Light Meter Test?

Adjustments:	ISO	1/f const.	Shutter Sp.	Histogram Accptble?
Shot 2				

Notes:

General Notes:
Photographer:
Sheet Number:

Settings HintS:

1/f :	4.0	11	22	varies w/ lens
Notes:	wide open	Midway	small open	
	max DF	Midway	least DF	

Shutter:	1200+	500	125	30	0"8
	Super Duper Fast	V. Fast	Fast	Slow	Sloooow
	Freezes Action to Capture Movement			hand held limit	Tripod!!!

Notes:
1. Based on Enviro Pick ISO 2. For Given ISO Select 1/f for Enviroment 3. Select Shutter Speed for Desired Effects 4. Check Meter + Shoot
5. Post shot REDO (1) to (4) based on Histogram Results 6. Take Shot and Document Histogram Result (Pos. or Neg.) 7. Document General No

21

Contact Info: serpa.c68322@gmail.com

Sheet Type II

integral Art concepts

Sheet Type II – Experiments with Set 1/f and Variable Shutter/ISO

Page No. _____

Picture No.
Picture Idea:
Date:
Conditions:
Location:

Initial ISO:
1/f :
Shutter spd:
Light Meter Test?

Adjustments:	ISO	1/f const.	Shutter Sp.	Histogram Accptble?
Shot 2				

Notes:

Picture No.
Picture Idea:
Date:
Conditions:
Location:

Initial ISO:
1/f :
Shutter spd:
Light Meter Test?

Adjustments:	ISO	1/f const.	Shutter Sp.	Histogram Accptble?
Shot 2				

Notes:

Picture No.
Picture Idea:
Date:
Conditions:
Location:

Initial ISO:
1/f :
Shutter spd:
Light Meter Test?

Adjustments:	ISO	1/f const.	Shutter Sp.	Histogram Accptble?
Shot 2				

Notes:

Picture No.
Picture Idea:
Date:
Conditions:
Location:

Initial ISO:
1/f :
Shutter spd:
Light Meter Test?

Adjustments:	ISO	1/f const.	Shutter Sp.	Histogram Accptble?
Shot 2				

Notes:

General Notes:
Photographer:
Sheet Number:

Settings HintS:

1/f :	4.0	11	22	varies w/ lens
	wide open	Midway	small open	
Notes:	max DF	Midway	least DF	

Shutter:	1200+	500	125	30	0"8
	Super Duper Fast	V. Fast	Fast	Slow	Sloooow
	Freezes Action to Capture Movement			hand held limit	Tripod!!!

Notes:

1. Based on Enviro Pick ISO 2. For Given ISO Select 1/f for Enviroment 3. Select Shutter Speed for Desired Effects 4. Check Meter + Shoot
5. Post shot REDO (1) to (4) based on Histogram Results 6. Take Shot and Document Histogram Result (Pos. or Neg.) 7. Document General No

www.flickr.com/photos/polite_engr

Last Revised: 9/13/2010

Sheet Type II

integral Art concepts

Sheet Type II - Experiments with Set 1/f and Variable Shutter/ISO   Page No. _____

Picture No.			Date:
Picture Idea:			Conditions:
			Location:

Initial ISO:
1/f :
Shutter spd:

Light Meter Test?

Adjustments:	ISO	1/f const.	Shutter Sp.	Histogram Accptble?
Shot 2				

Notes:

Picture No.			Date:
Picture Idea:			Conditions:
			Location:

Initial ISO:
1/f :
Shutter spd:

Light Meter Test?

Adjustments:	ISO	1/f const.	Shutter Sp.	Histogram Accptble?
Shot 2				

Notes:

Picture No.			Date:
Picture Idea:			Conditions:
			Location:

Initial ISO:
1/f :
Shutter spd:

Light Meter Test?

Adjustments:	ISO	1/f const.	Shutter Sp.	Histogram Accptble?
Shot 2				

Notes:

Picture No.			Date:
Picture Idea:			Conditions:
			Location:

Initial ISO:
1/f :
Shutter spd:

Light Meter Test?

Adjustments:	ISO	1/f const.	Shutter Sp.	Histogram Accptble?
Shot 2				

Notes:

General Notes:
Photographer:
Sheet Number:

Settings HintS:

1/f :	4.0	11	22	varies w/ lens
Notes:	wide open	Midway	small open	
	max DF	Midway	least DF	

Notes:

Shutter:	1200+	500	125	30	0"8
	Super Duper Fast	V. Fast	Fast	Slow	Slooow
	Freezes Action to Capture Movement			hand held limit	Tripod!!!

1. Based on Enviro Pick ISO   2. For Given ISO Select 1/f for Enviroment   3. Select Shutter Speed for Desired Effects   4. Check Meter + Shoot

5. Post shot REDO (1) to (4) based on Histogram Results   6. Take Shot and Document Histogram Result (Pos. or Neg.)   7. Document General Nc

Last Revised: 9/13/2010   www.flickr.com/photos/polite_engr   Contact Info: serpa.c68322@gmail.com

Sheet Type III

Contact Info: serpa.c68322@gmail.com

www.flickr.com/photos/polite_engr

Last Revised 9/13/2010

integral Art concepts

Sheet Type III - Photography Log Sheet for Shot Construction and Documentation for Analysis

s of Shot Selection based on Setting Aperture and Compensating for Conditions with ISO and Shuter Speed [Note: Sheet is Applicable for ISO/shutter as Controllin{

Page No. ___

Shot No.	Lens (mm)	Selection of:			Light Meter Reading?	Post Shot:	General Notes on Each Shot:
		"f"	ISO	shutter speed	Basis of Selections:	Desc. Loc. & Rding:	Replicate Histogrm?
1			100 200 400 800 1600			-2 . . 1 . . + . . 1 . . 2		
2			100 200 400 800 1600			-2 . . 1 . . + . . 1 . . 2		
3			100 200 400 800 1600			-2 . . 1 . . + . . 1 . . 2		
4			100 200 400 800 1600			-2 . . 1 . . + . . 1 . . 2		
5			100 200 400 800 1600			-2 . . 1 . . + . . 1 . . 2		

Constants:

1. Location:
2. Date:
3. Time:
4: Light Description:
5. Description of Environment:

Story Board Shot:
Note Light Direction, Objects, People . . .

Sheet Type III

integral Art concepts

Page No.

Sheet Type III - Photography Log Sheet for Shot Construction and Documentation for Analysis

is of Shot Selection based on Setting Aperture and Compensating for Conditions with ISO and Shuter Speed [Note: Sheet is Applicable for ISO/shutter as Controllin

Shot No.	Lens (mm)	Selection of:			Light Meter Reading?		Post Shot:	General Notes on Each Shot:
		"f"	ISO	shutter speed	Basis of Selections:	Desc. Loc. & Rding:	Replicate Histogrm?	
1			100 200 400 800 1600			-2 .. 1 .. + .. 1 .. 2		
2			100 200 400 800 1600			-2 .. 1 .. + .. 1 .. 2		
3			100 200 400 800 1600			-2 .. 1 .. + .. 1 .. 2		
4			100 200 400 800 1600			-2 .. 1 .. + .. 1 .. 2		
5			100 200 400 800 1600			-2 .. 1 .. + .. 1 .. 2		

Constants:

1. Location:

2. Date:

3. Time:

4: Light Description:

5. Description of Environment:

Story Board Shot:
Note Light Direction, Objects, People . . .

Sheet Type III

integral Art concepts

Sheet Type III - Photography Log Sheet for Shot Construction and Documentation for Analysis   **Page No.**
s of Shot Selection based on Setting Aperture and Compensating for Conditions with ISO and Shuter Speed [Note: Sheet is Applicable for ISO/shutter as Controllin

Shot No.	Lens (mm)	Selection of:			Basis of Selections:	Light Meter Reading? Desc. Loc. & Rding:	Post Shot: Replicate Histogrm?	General Notes on Each Shot:
		"f"	ISO	shutter speed				
1			100 200 400 800 1600			-2..1..+..1..2		
2			100 200 400 800 1600			-2..1..+..1..2		
3			100 200 400 800 1600			-2..1..+..1..2		
4			100 200 400 800 1600			-2..1..+..1..2		
5			100 200 400 800 1600			-2..1..+..1..2		

Constants:
1. Location:
2. Date:
3. Time:
4: Light Description:
5. Description of Environment:

Story Board Shot:
Note Light Direction, Objects, People . . .

www.flickr.com/photos/polite_engr

Contact Info: serpa c68322@gmail.com

Last Revised: 9/13/2010

Sheet Type IV

Contact Info: serpa.c68322@gmail.com

www.flickr.com/photos/polite_engr

Last Revised: 9/13/2010

integral Art concepts

Sheet Type IV - Photography Log Sheet for Documenting Mechanics of Photographic Flow of Work

Page No.

Shot No.	Date	Time	Lens(mm)	Description of:			Selection of:			Light Meter Reading?		Post Shot:	
				Light	Enviroment	"f"	ISO	"s"	Basis of Selections:	Desc. Loc. & Rding:		Replicate Histogrm, Accept?	
							100 200 400 800 1600			-2 . . 1 . . + . . 1 . . 2			
Shot Location:					Gen. Note:								
							100 200 400 800 1600			-2 . . 1 . . + . . 1 . . 2			
Shot Location:					Gen. Note:								
							100 200 400 800 1600			-2 . . 1 . . + . . 1 . . 2			
Shot Location:					Gen. Note:								
							100 200 400 800 1600			-2 . . 1 . . + . . 1 . . 2			
Shot Location:					Gen. Note:								
							100 200 400 800 1600			-2 . . 1 . . + . . 1 . . 2			
Shot Location:					Gen. Note:								

Sheet Type IV

Created By: B Serpa | ***integral Art concepts*** | Copyrighted By: B Serpa

Sheet Type IV - Photography Log Sheet for Documenting Mechanics of Photographic Flow of Work **Page No.**

				Description of:		Selection of:				Light Meter Reading?	Post Shot:
Shot No.	Date	Time	Lens(mm)	Light	Enviroment	"f"	ISO	"s"	Basis of Selections:	Desc. Loc. & Rding:	Replicate Histogrm, Accept?
							100 200 400 800 1600			-2 . . 1 . . + . . 1 . . 2	
Shot Location:					Gen. Note:						
							100 200 400 800 1600			-2 . . 1 . . + . . 1 . . 2	
Shot Location:					Gen. Note:						
							100 200 400 800 1600			-2 . . 1 . . + . . 1 . . 2	
Shot Location:					Gen. Note:						
							100 200 400 800 1600			-2 . . 1 . . + . . 1 . . 2	
Shot Location:					Gen. Note:						
							100 200 400 800 1600			-2 . . 1 . . + . . 1 . . 2	
Shot Location:					Gen. Note:						

Last Revised: 9/13/2010 | **www.flickr.com/photos/polite_engr** | *Contact Info: serpa.c68322@gmail.com*

ABOUT THE AUTHOR

An engineer by trade/schooling.
Amateur dreamer by default.
Admirer of minimalism and simplicity.
Adventurer in the safest of ways.
And most of all intellectually curious;
Always chasing the right answer.